Early
Learning
Centre

my first dictionary

note to parents

Explain to your child how a dictionary works.
Talk about the alphabetical order of the words.
Point to the highlighted letters at the top and bottom of the pages
and explain how these help us to find words more quickly.
Find some familiar words and talk about the pictures and the definitions.
Soon your child will have fun looking up words for him/herself.

written by Jock Graham and Marie Lister
Illustrated by Jeannette Slater
designed by Liz Auger

dinosaur

First published in 1995 for Early Learning Centre
by World International Limited, Deanway Technology Centre,
Handforth, Cheshire SK9 3FB. Printed in Great Britain.
ISBN 0 7498 2381 X

Aa

address
Your address is the number of your house, the street, the town and the country that you live in.

aeroplane
An aeroplane is a big machine that has wings and an engine. It flies in the air and takes people from one place to another.

afraid
When you are afraid, something has scared or frightened you.

afternoon
Afternoon is from 12 o'clock in the middle of the day till 5 or 6 o'clock in the evening.

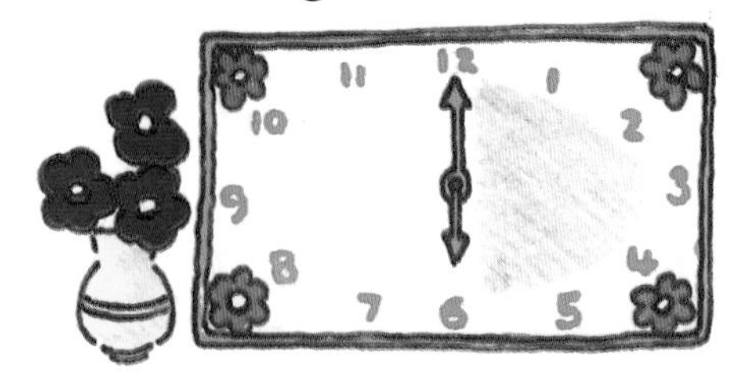

age
Your age is the number of years from when you were born till now.

agree
If you agree with what somebody says, you think they are right.

alphabet
The alphabet is the list of all the 26 letters in the English language. It begins with a,b,c.

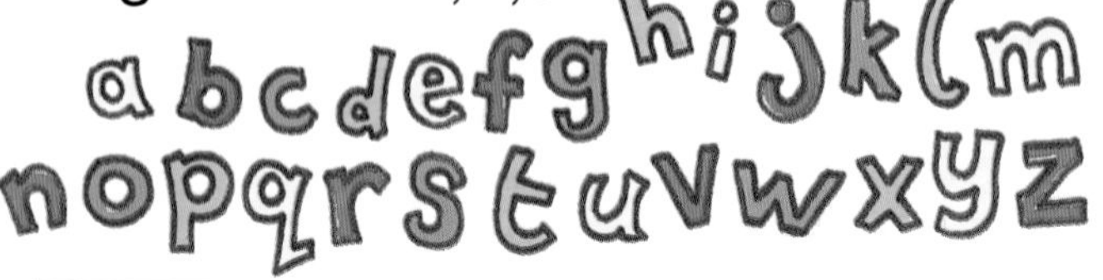

ambulance
An ambulance takes sick people to and from the hospital.

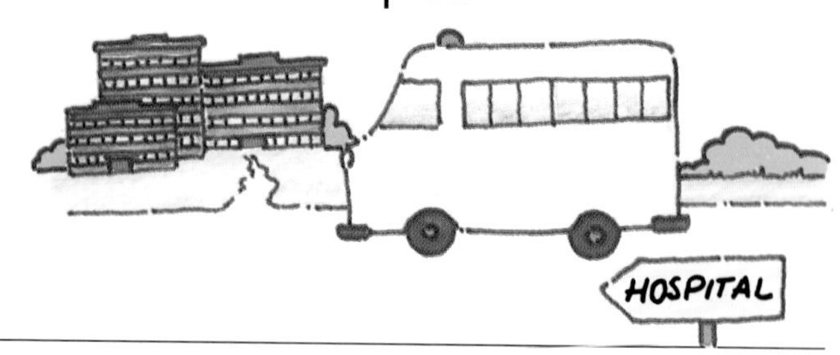

angry
Angry is how you feel when something annoys you and you lose your temper.

ankle

Your ankle is the part of your body where your leg joins your foot.

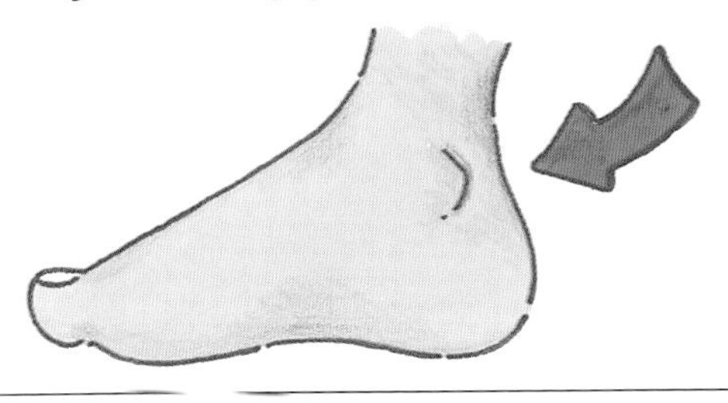

answer

If somebody asks you a question and you know the answer, you can tell them what they want to know.

ant

An ant is a very small insect that can carry things much bigger than itself. Ants can bite!

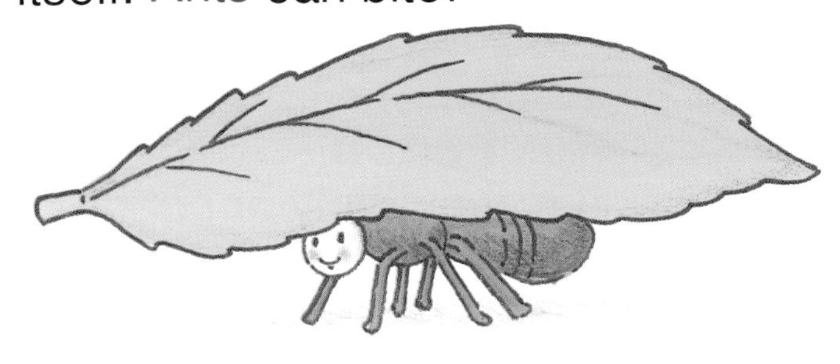

apple

An apple is a hard, round, juicy fruit that grows on trees. Its skin can be red, green or yellow.

arm

The part of your body from your shoulder to your hand is your arm

ask

Ask a question if there is anything you want to know.

asleep

When you are asleep your eyes are closed and sometimes you dream.

autumn

In autumn the leaves fall off the trees.

awake

Being awake means having your eyes open and knowing what is happening around you.

Bb

baby

A baby is a very small boy or girl that has just been born. There are baby animals too.

bad

People are bad when they do naughty or nasty things. Fruit is bad when it's too old to eat.

bag

A bag is used for carrying things. It can be made of plastic, paper or leather.

balloon

A balloon is a thin rubber bag. Fill it with air and it will get bigger and float away.

banana

A banana is a fruit with a thick yellow skin. Monkeys love bananas!

bark

Bark is a word for the loud noise a dog makes. Bark is also the outside of a tree.

bathroom

In a bathroom, there is usually a sink, a bath, and a toilet.

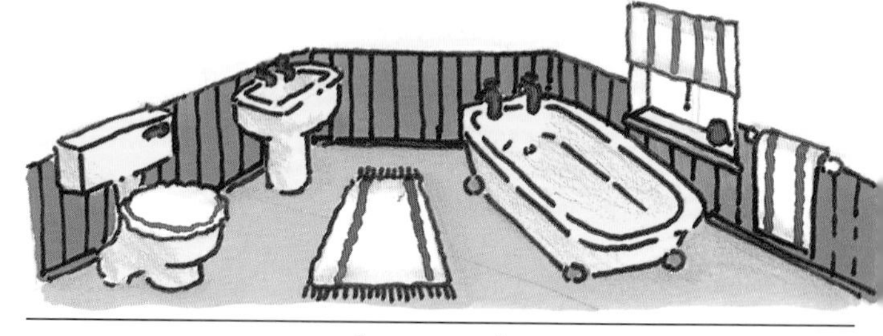

beach

The beach is the sandy or pebbly land next to the sea.

bed

A bed is something you sleep in.

bee

A bee is a flying insect that makes honey from the special powder it collects from flowers.

bicycle

A bicycle has two wheels that go round when you push the pedals with your feet.

big

Big is a word used to tell you the size of something. Your father is much bigger than you.

bird

A bird has two wings and a beak and is covered in feathers. Almost all birds can fly. Birds lay eggs.

birthday

Your birthday is the day of the year when you were born.

boat

A boat is used for travelling across water. A boat is smaller than a ship.

body

This picture gives the names of some parts of the body.

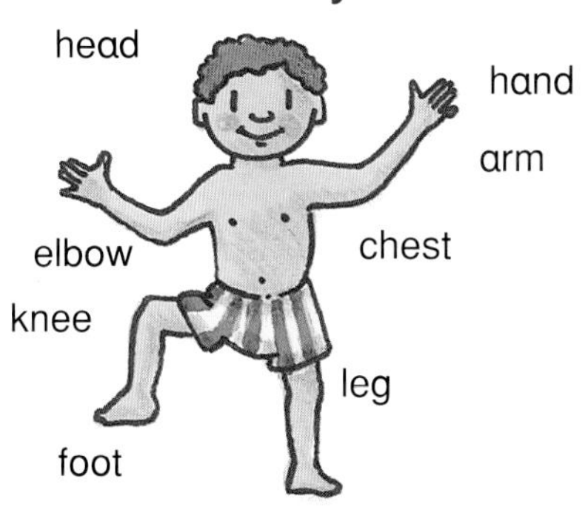

book

A book has paper pages with lots of words, and sometimes pictures, printed on them.

box

A box is made to hold things. It usually has four sides, a bottom and a top or lid.

boy
A boy grows up to be a man. Your father used to be a boy.

branch
A branch is like an arm that grows out of the main part of a tree.

bread
Bread is made from flour, and is used for sandwiches or toast.

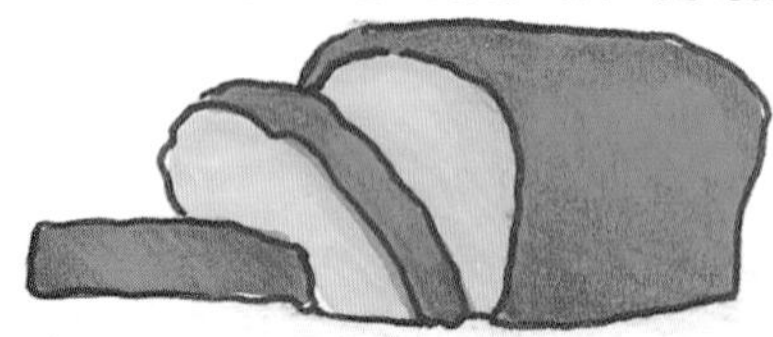

break
If you kick a football against a window, it will break the glass.

brush
Different kinds of brush are used for hair, teeth, nails, painting, and sweeping up.

building
A building has walls, a roof and a floor. Houses, offices, schools and churches are buildings.

bump
When you bump into someone, you walk or run into them.

burn
Many things burn when they get too hot or are touched by a flame.

bus
A bus has lots of seats and travels on the road. We get on or off at a bus stop.

Cc

cake

A cake is made from eggs, flour, butter and sugar. You get one on your birthday.

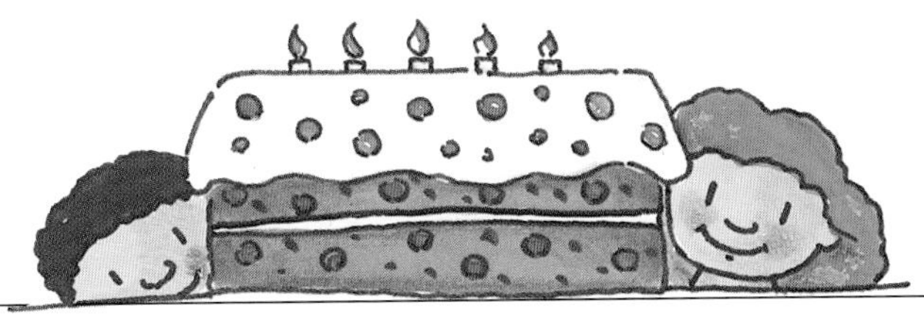

camera

A camera is used for taking photographs or moving pictures of things or people.

car

A car has an engine, four wheels and seats for four or five people. It travels on the road.

carry

If you carry something, you lift it up and take it somewhere else.

cat

A cat is a furry animal with four legs, a tail and sharp claws. Lions and tigers are big cats.

catch

When I throw the ball to you, you should use both hands to catch it.

chair

A chair is a seat for one person.

chase

You chase someone when you run after them and try to catch them.

cheese

Cheese is made from the milk of cows, sheep or goats. It can be soft or hard.

chicken

A chicken is a bird which lays eggs. Its baby is a chick.

children

Young boys and girls are known as children

clean

When you clean something, you get all the dirt off it.

clever

Someone who knows the answers to lots of questions is very clever

climb

When you climb, you use your hands and feet to get up to the top.

clock

A clock is a machine that tells us the time. It is bigger than a watch.

clothes

Clothes are things we wear to keep us dry and warm.

cold

When you are cold you are not warm enough. Put on some thicker clothes!

colour

There are seven different colours in a rainbow.

computer

A computer is a machine that can work out lots of things very quickly – even hard sums!

cook

You cook foods by heating them up. You can fry, bake, boil, grill or microwave them!

count

When you count you say numbers one after another.

cow

A cow is a big animal that lives on a farm and gives us milk.

crash

When one car hits another one by accident, we say they crash

cross

When you cross the road, you walk from one side to the other.

cry

When we cry, salty tears come from our eyes. We are upset.

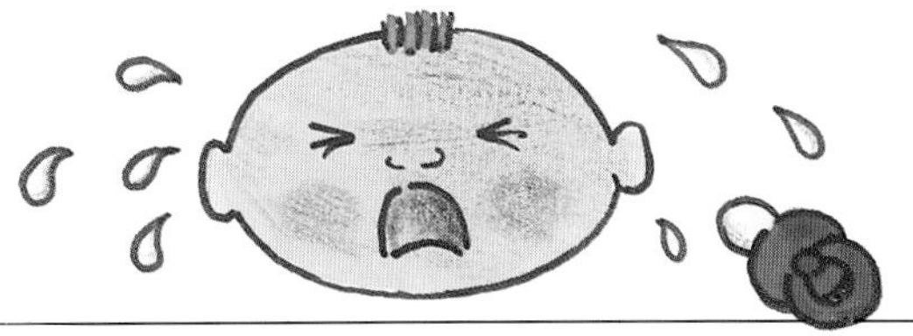

curtain

A curtain is a cloth that hangs by a window. We close the curtains at night.

cut

When you cut yourself you break your skin and blood comes out.

Dd

dark

It is dark when the sun goes down or when there is no light to see by.

day

A day is a length of time. There are seven days in a week.

dictionary

A dictionary is a book that tells us what words mean. This is your dictionary!

different

When two things are different, they are not the same.

dig

You can make a big hole in the sand if you dig with your spade.

dinosaur

A dinosaur is a very big animal that lived millions of years ago. There are none alive today.

dirty

If you are dirty it means you are not clean and you need a bath!

do

Instead of just sitting here all day, let's go out and do something exciting!

doctor

A doctor is a person who knows how to make you better when you are ill.

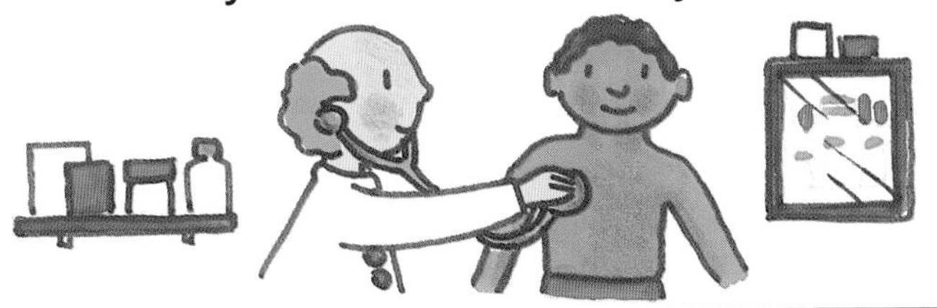

dog

A dog is a hairy animal with four legs and a tail. Many people keep them as pets.

door

When we leave the house or the car we lock the doors so that no one can get in.

down

When you go from the top of the stairs to the bottom, you are going down.

draw

When you draw something you make a picture of what it looks like. We call this picture a drawing.

drink

Lemonade, orange juice, tea and coffee are drinks. We drink when we are thirsty.

drop

If you drop a plate, it will fall to the floor and break.

dry

You can use a hat to keep your hair dry when you are out in the rain.

duck

A duck is a bird that has special feet for swimming in the water.

Ee

ear
You have two ears, one on each side of your head. You use them to hear with.

easy
Something that is easy is not hard to do.

eat
You eat food. You put it in your mouth, chew it and swallow it.

egg
An egg has a hard outside, and a soft inside. Eggs are laid by birds.

elephant
An elephant is a huge grey animal with big ears, white tusks, and a long nose called a trunk.

empty
Something is empty if there is nothing inside it.

evening
Evening is the time of day after 5 o'clock and when you eat your evening meal.

exciting
It's very exciting to open your presents on Christmas Day. You don't know what you might find!

eye
We look at things with our eyes. What colour are your eyes?

Ff

face
Your face is the front of your head, where your eyes, nose and mouth are.

fall
Leaves fall from trees and drop to the ground in autumn.

family
Your mother and father, your brothers and sisters, and all your other relations are your family.

farm
A farm is a big piece of land where a farmer keeps animals or grows plants for food.

fast
A fast car is one that can go really quickly.

fat
If you eat too much, you will get fat and will be heavier than you should be.

father
Your father is older and bigger than you. He is one of your parents.

find
When you find something, you have been looking for it.

finger
We have four fingers and a thumb on each hand.

fire
We can burn coal, wood or gas in a fire to keep ourselves warm.

fish
A fish is an animal that lives and can breathe in water.

flower
The flower is the brightly-coloured part of a plant which we pick.

foot
Your foot is at the end of your leg. Feet are what we stand on.

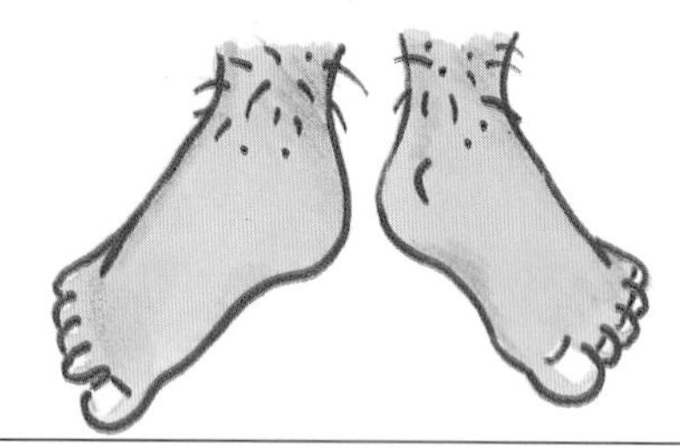

football
In football, two teams of eleven players try to score goals by kicking a ball into a net.

fork
We can eat with a fork. A fork has points at the end which we use to pick up food.

friend
A friend is a person you like a lot but who is not part of your family.

frighten
If you make someone afraid by pulling scary faces at them, you frighten them.

fruit
Apples, oranges and bananas are different kinds of fruit. Fruit grows on trees or bushes.

full
A cup or glass is full when you can't get any more into it.

Gg

game

A game is something that you play which has rules. You can play for fun or play to win!

garden

Some houses have land called a garden where you can grow grass, flowers or vegetables.

gate

A gate is a kind of door for a garden wall or fence.

gerbil

A gerbil is a small furry animal that people keep as a pet. It sleeps during the day and plays at night.

giant

In stories, a very tall or huge person is called a giant.

girl

A girl grows up to be a woman. Your mother used to be a girl.

give

When you give something to someone you let them have it.

glass

You can see through glass. It feels smooth and breaks easily! Windows are made of glass.

glove

A glove is something you wear on your hand to keep it warm. Do you have a pair of gloves?

go
When you go somewhere, you move from where you are to another place.

goat
A goat is a small animal with horns. Goats give milk and are kept on farms.

good
A good person is kind to other people. A good book is one that you enjoy reading.

grandfather
You have two grandfathers. One is your mother's father, and one is your father's father.

grandmother
Your mother's mother and your father's mother are your grandmothers.

grass
Grass is a green plant that you can walk on. Golf, football and other games are played on grass.

ground
Grass, trees and plants all grow in the ground, which is the surface of the Earth.

grow
All living things grow. People grow. You will grow bigger as you get older.

guess
If you do not know the answer to the question, you can sometimes make a guess.

Hh

hair
People have hair on their heads; animals often have hair all over.

hand
Your fingers and thumb are on your hand, on the end of your arm.

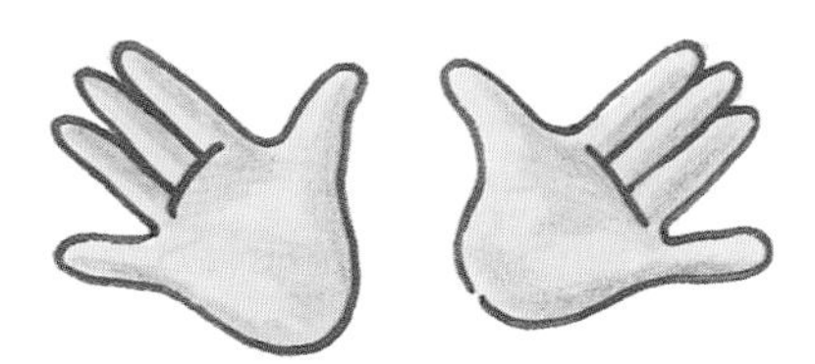

happy
If you are happy you are feeling cheerful and not sad at all. Hope you have a happy birthday!

head
Your face is at the front of your head, and your hair is on the top, back and sides.

hear
We use our ears to hear what people are saying.

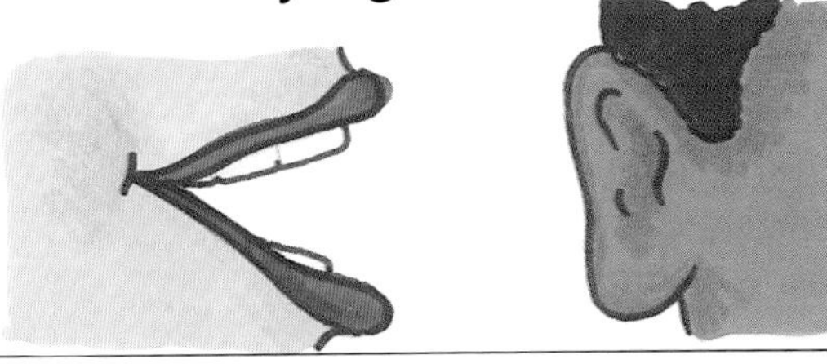

heavy
A heavy box weighs a lot and is difficult to lift or carry.

help
If you help someone, you do part of the work – such as helping with the washing-up.

hide
You hide when you go to a place where nobody can find you.

high
A mountain is high because its top is a long way above the ground.

hit

If you hit a ball with a bat it sometimes goes a long way!

holiday

A holiday is a time when people take a rest from work or school.

horse

A horse is a big animal with four legs that people ride for fun or in races.

hospital

A hospital is a building where doctors and nurses look after people who are ill.

hot

When the sun shines brightly, it feels hot outside.

hour

An hour is used to measure time. There are 24 hours in a day.

house

Your house is the building where you live with your family.

hungry

When you have not eaten anything for a long time, you get really hungry.

hurt

If you hurt yourself, you feel pain.

Ii

ice

Ice is water that has frozen hard.

ice-cream

Ice-cream is made from frozen milk and comes in lots of flavours.

in

If you stay in the house, you don't go out.

insect

An insect is a small animal with six legs.

Jj

jeans

Jeans are trousers that are made of a cloth called denim.

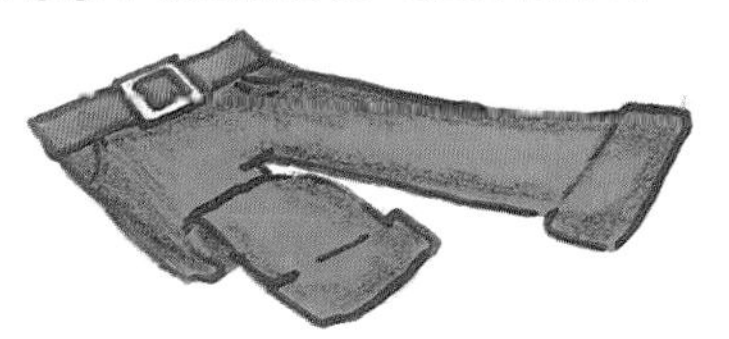

jigsaw

A jigsaw is a puzzle made of pieces that fit together in a special way.

job

Your job is what you do when you go to work.

juice

Juice is the liquid that can be squeezed out of food. Fruit juice is good for you.

jump

You jump by pushing both feet off the ground at once.

Kk

keep

Can you keep a secret and not tell anyone else?

kettle

We boil water in a kettle so we can make hot drinks!

key

A key opens locks on things such as doors and suitcases. It is made in a special shape.

kick

Swing your leg and hit the ball with your foot – that's how to kick!

kind

People are kind when they do or say nice things.

kitchen

The kitchen is the room in a house where all the cooking and washing-up is done.

knee

Your knee is the part of your leg that makes it bend in the middle.

knife

A knife has a sharp edge for cutting things.

know

You know something when you remember it or understand how to do it. Do you know how to swim?

Ll

ladder

A ladder is used for climbing up to high places we cannot reach.

late

If you are late getting home, you should have got there earlier.

laugh

If we hear a very funny joke, we laugh out loud.

leaf

A leaf is the flat green part growing on a plant or the branch of a tree.

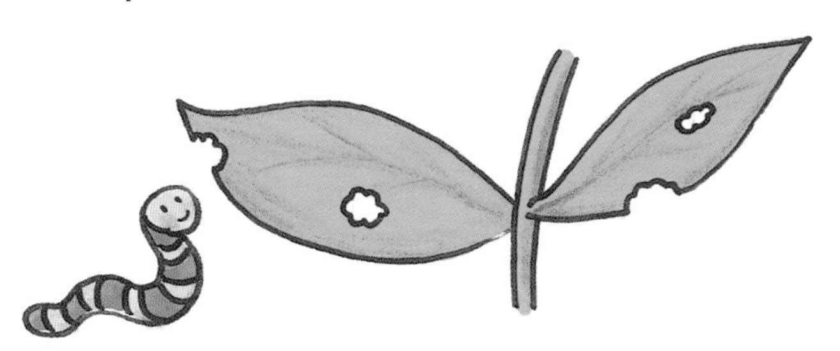

learn

You learn to do things by listening carefully to your parent or teacher, and by practising.

left

We read English from left to right. We look left and right when we cross the road.

leg

Your legs are the parts of your body on which you stand, walk and run.

letter

There are 26 letters used in the English language. They are called the alphabet.

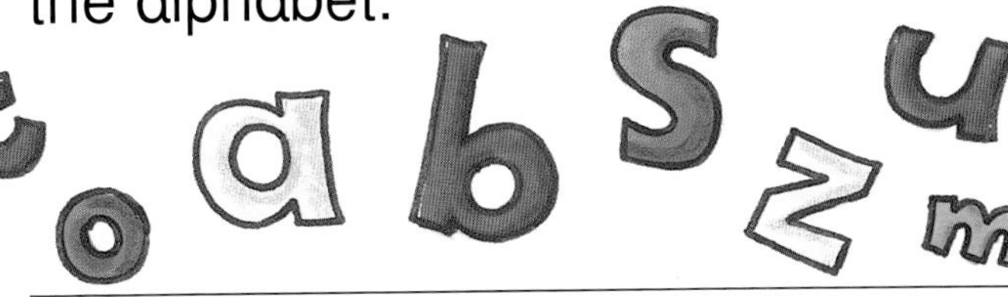

letter

A letter is a written message that you send to someone.

lift
A strong man can lift up a very heavy weight.

light
Light comes from the sun and from light bulbs. Light makes it possible for us to see.

light
A piece of paper is so light that it is very easy to pick up.

like
People like doing things that they enjoy. They also like their friends and family.

lion
A lion is a strong, fierce wild animal that lives in Africa.

listen
You listen to somebody when you want to hear what they are saying.

little
Little is the same as small. It means not very big.

live
If you are lucky, you could live to be 100 years old!

loud
A sound is loud if you can hear it from a long way away.

Mm

machine

A machine can be used for making things. Cars and buses are machines too.

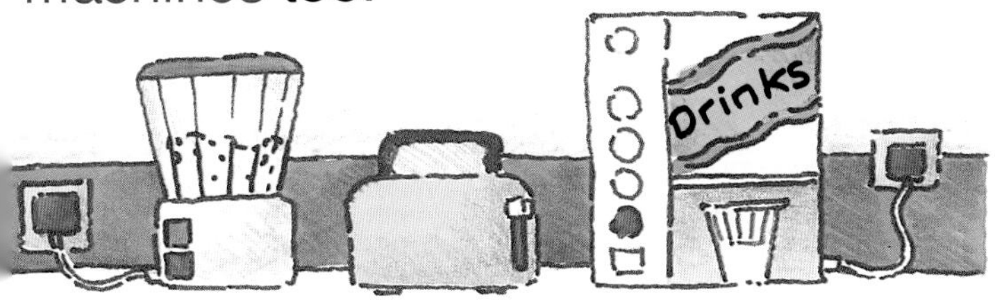

magic

If somebody says some strange words and you turn into a frog – that's magic!

make

You can make a big tower from lots of little bricks.

man

A man is a boy who has grown up and is at least 18 years old.

map

A map is a drawing of a place as if you are looking at it from high in the air.

market

A market is a place where you can buy and sell things.

match

When two teams play a match, each one tries to score the most points.

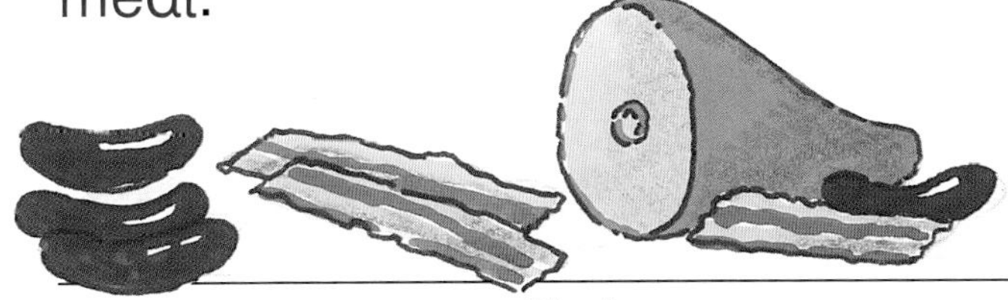

meat

The parts of animals and birds which we cook and eat are called meat.

medicine

Medicine is what the doctor gives you to make you well again when you are ill.

meet

People meet when they arrive at the same time in the same place.

mend

You mend something by putting it back together.

milk

Milk is a liquid that often comes from cows. We pour it on our cornflakes.

million

One million is a very big number. We write it like this: 1,000,000.

minute

A minute is an amount of time. There are 60 minutes in every hour.

mirror

A mirror is a piece of glass that you can see yourself in.

mix

When you mix blue paint and yellow paint, you get green paint!

money

Metal coins and paper notes are money. We use money to buy things.

monkey

A monkey is an animal that has long arms. Some monkeys also have long tails.

month

A month is an amount of time. There are twelve months in every year.

moon

You can see the moon in the sky. It is very bright at night.

morning

Morning is the name for the hours from when you wake up until the middle of the day.

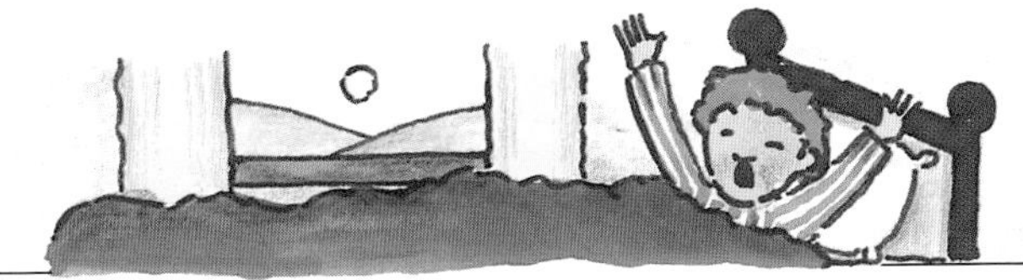

mother

A mother is a woman who has children. How many children does your mother have?

mountain

A mountain is a very high hill. You can see a long way from the top.

mouse

A mouse is a little animal with a long tail. It can live in fields or in buildings.

mouth

Your mouth is below your nose. You use your mouth to eat, speak and breathe.

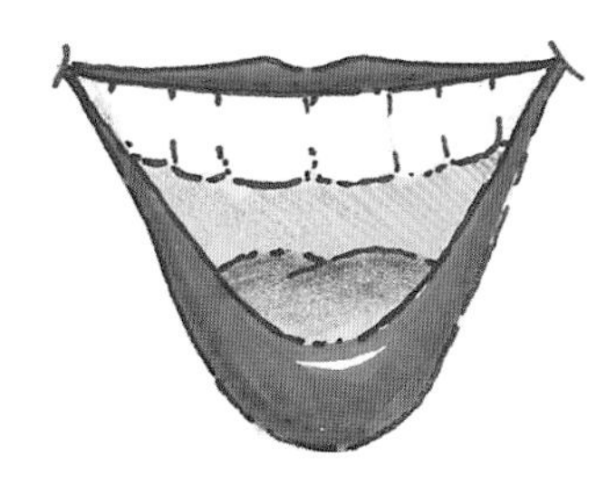

move

If something can move, it can go (or be taken) from one place to another.

music

Songs that people sing and tunes that they play are called music.

Nn

name

Your name is what everybody calls you. It was given to you when you were born.

naughty

If you know you are doing something wrong, you are being naughty.

near

When we are near something or somebody, we are not far away from them.

neck

Your head is joined to the rest of your body by your neck.

nest

A nest is a place where birds lay their eggs and feed their babies.

net

Boats go out to sea and catch fish in a net.

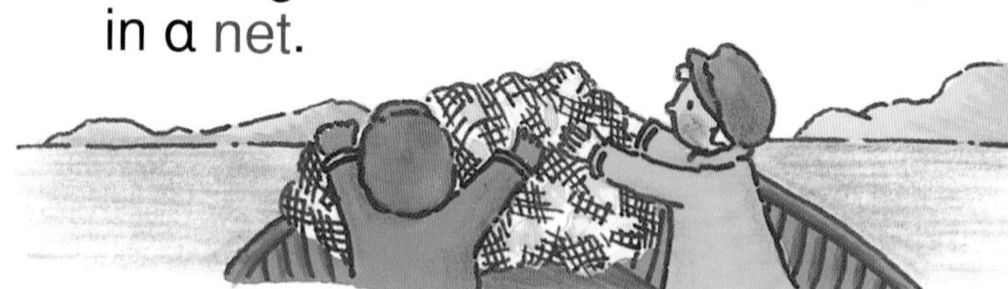

never

If you have never been swimming, you have not done it once in your whole life.

new

When we have just bought something, it is new. When we do something new, we have never done it before.

newspaper

A newspaper is full of stories about interesting things that have happened.

nice

If you are nice to people, you are kind and friendly. Things that you enjoy are nice to do.

night

Night is the name for the hours when it is dark and people are asleep.

no

You say no thank you when you don't want something.

noise

The noise of something is the sound that it makes. Children make a lot of noise!

nose

Your nose is between your eyes and your mouth. You use it to breathe through.

now

Doing something now means doing it straight away and not waiting until later. We can cross the road now.

number

Numbers are what you use when you count or do sums.

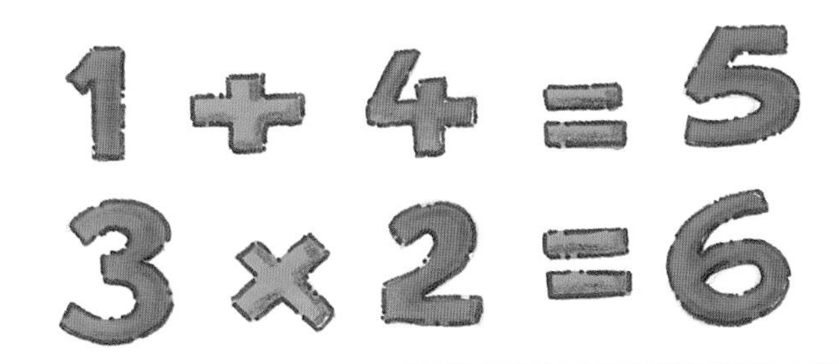

nurse

A nurse is a man or woman who looks after people who are ill. Most nurses work in hospitals.

nut

A nut is a kind of hard fruit that grows on trees or bushes.

Oo

off
You take your jacket off when you get hot. You get off the bus when it gets to your stop.

old
A person who was born a long time ago is old. Old things were made a long time ago.

once
If you do something once, you have done it one time.

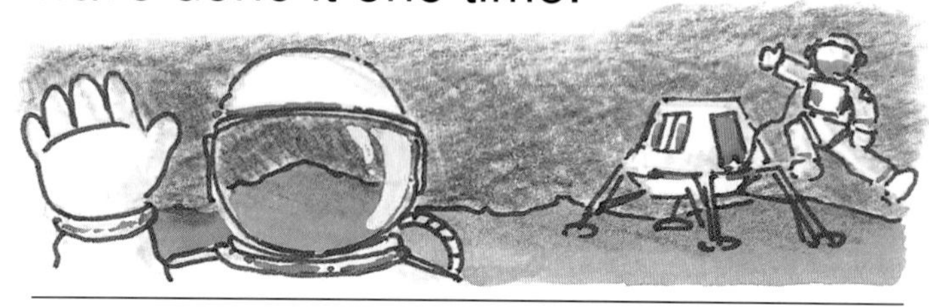

onion
An onion is a round white vegetable. When you peel an onion it makes your eyes water!

open
You open a box to look inside.

opposite
If two things are opposites, they are very different.

orange
An orange is a round, brightly-coloured fruit that grows on trees. Peel off the skin before you eat it!

out
If you go out you leave the house.

owl
An owl is a bird with very big eyes that it uses to see in the dark.

Pp

paddle
You paddle in the sea when you walk in the water where it is very shallow.

page
Each side of every piece of paper in a book is called a page.

paint
Paint is a coloured liquid used to make a picture or to colour things.

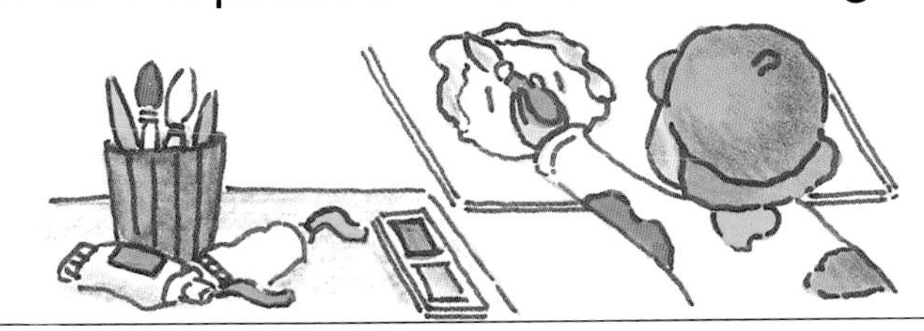

paper
Paper is used for books and for wrapping parcels. It is made from trees.

park
A park is an open place with grass and trees, where anybody can go and play.

party
At a party your friends eat food and dance to music.

path
A path is a kind of pavement in a park or garden.

pavement
The pavement is the part of the street where people can safely walk.

pea
A pea is a small, round, green vegetable that grows in a pod.

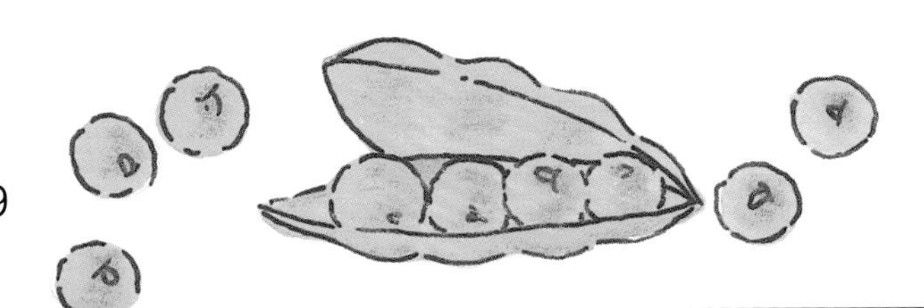

pen
A pen is filled with ink. You use it to write with.

pencil
A pencil makes grey marks on paper that you can rub out. Coloured pencils make coloured marks.

photograph
A photograph is a picture taken by a camera and printed on special paper.

picture
A picture can be a drawing, a painting, a photograph, or a film we watch at the cinema.

pie
A pie is meat, fruit or vegetables baked in pastry.

pig
A pig is a fat farm animal with a big nose called a snout, and a curly tail.

pillow
When we are in bed, we rest our head on a soft pillow.

pin
A pin is a small piece of metal with a flat head and a sharp point.

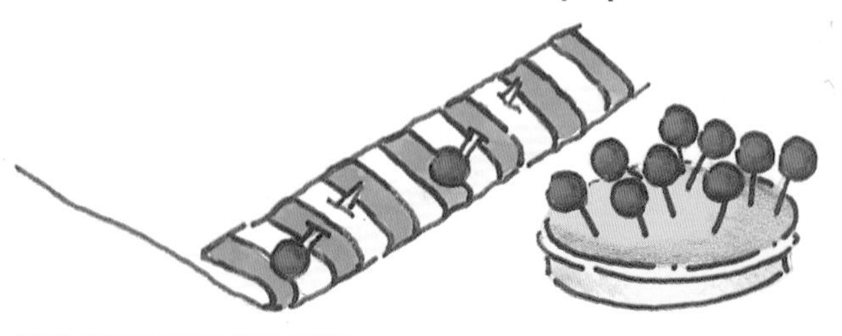

plant
A plant is a living thing that grows in the ground or in plant pots.

plate

A plate is a flat dish that holds food.

play

When you play you are having a game or doing something for fun.

pocket

A pocket is like a little bag sewn into your clothes. You can carry things in your pockets.

point

If you want someone to notice something you use your finger to point it out.

postman

A postman is a person whose job is to deliver letters and parcels.

potato

A potato is a round white vegetable with a thin brown skin on the outside.

pram

A pram is like a baby's bed with four wheels and a handle to push it with.

present

A present is something you are given at Christmas or on your birthday.

pull

If a door says pull you move it towards you.

puppet

A puppet is a toy moved by strings or worn like a glove on your hand.

purse

You can keep your money in a little bag called a purse.

push

If a door says push, you move it away from you.

pyjamas

Your pyjamas are the jacket and trousers that you wear in bed.

Qq

queen

The queen is the most important woman in a royal family.

question

If you want to know about something, you can ask someone a question about it.

queue

A queue is a long line of people who are waiting for something.

quick

If you want to be quick you have to do things in a very short time.

quiet

A thing or person that makes very little noise is quiet.

Rr

rabbit

A rabbit is a small furry animal with long ears.

race

The quickest person in a race is the one who finishes first.

railway

Trains and the track they run on are called a railway. Trains stop at railway stations.

rain

Drops of water that fall from clouds in the sky are called rain.

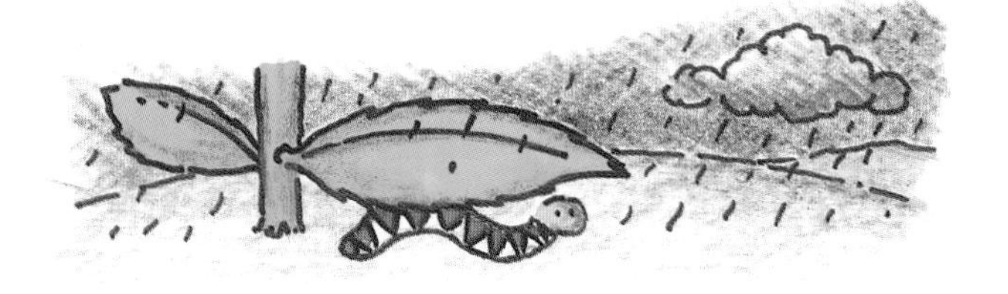

read

If you can look at the words on this page and understand them, you can read.

rest

When you have a rest you stop what you are doing for a while.

ride

You can ride your bicycle. You sit on it and pedal it with your feet.

right

Most people use their right hand to write with.

right

"What is 1 + 1?" "The right answer is 2."

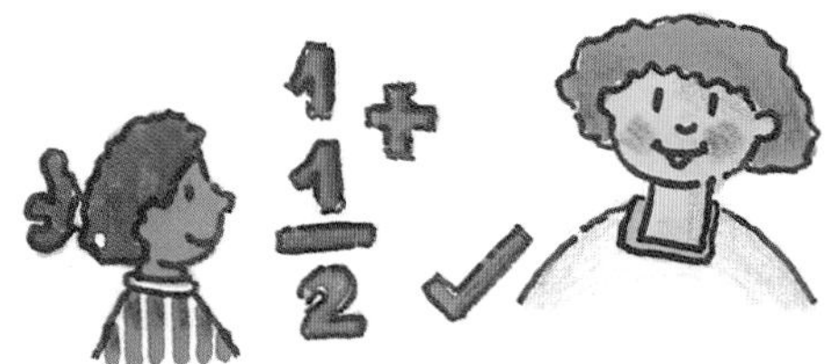

ring

A ring is a band you can wear on your finger.

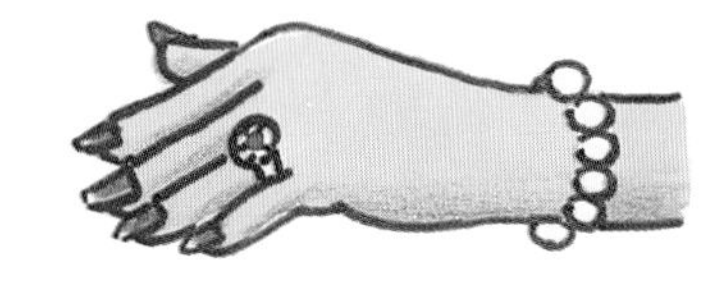

river

A river is a long strip of fresh water which flows across the land to the sea.

road

A road is a wide, hard track for cars and buses to drive on.

roof

The roof is the top part of a building which keeps the rain and snow out.

room

A room usually has four walls, a ceiling, a floor and a door. It may have windows too.

rose

A rose is a flower with soft petals and thorns.

round

Anything in the shape of a circle or ball is round.

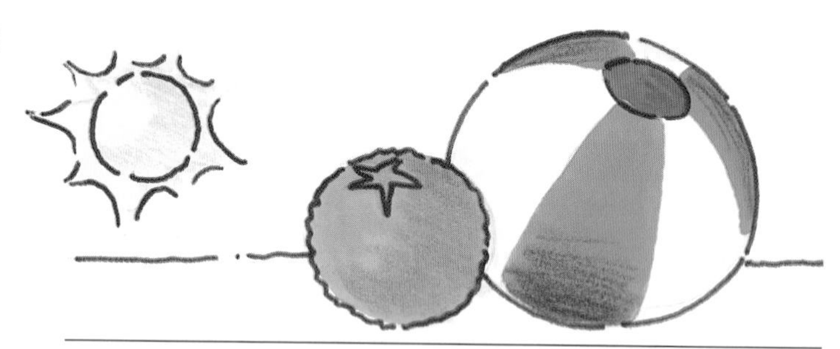

ruler

We can use a ruler to measure things.

run

When you run you go faster than when you walk.

Ss

sad

A sad story is one that makes you cry or feel upset.

salt

Salt is a white powder that some people put on their food.

sand

Sand is tiny crushed pieces of rock. A beach at the seaside is often sandy.

say

When you open your mouth and speak, people can hear the words you say.

school

A school is a place where you go to learn things from teachers.

sea

When you go to the beach, the salty water that you paddle in is the sea.

second

A second is a very short length of time. There are 60 seconds in a minute.

see

If your eyes are open and you are looking at this page, you can see the pictures.

shadow

A shadow is the dark shape of something that is put in front of a light.

shake
Lemonade goes really fizzy when you shake it up and down or from side to side.

share
If you share something, you let someone have part of it.

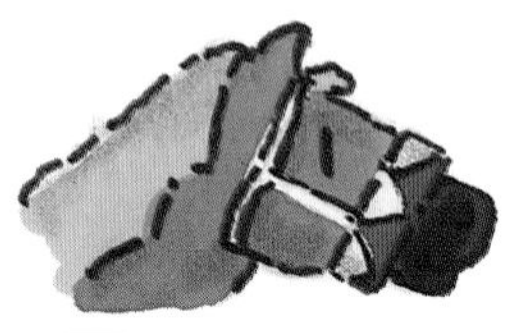

sharp
A knife cuts things easily because it has a sharp edge.

sheep
A sheep is an animal that lives on a farm. Sheep have woolly coats that we make clothes from.

shell
Some animals, such as crabs, turtles and snails, have shells.

shine
If the clouds go away, the sun will shine and the sky will get brighter.

ship
A ship travels across the sea. Most ships have engines, but some use sails that catch the wind.

shirt
A shirt covers the top half of your body. We often wear a shirt and tie as school uniform.

shoe
You wear a shoe on each foot to keep your feet warm and dry.

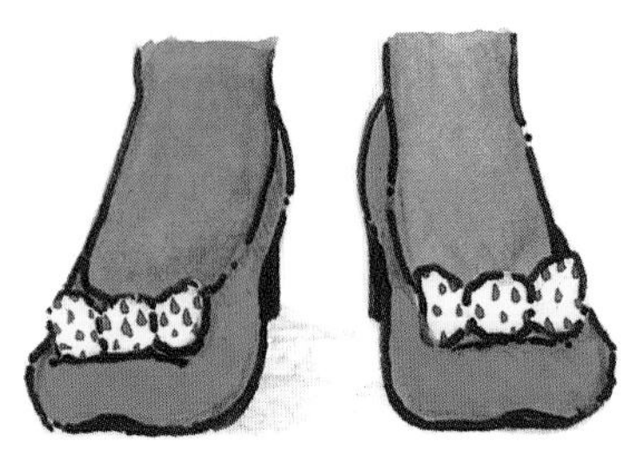

shop

A shop is a place that sells things. A chemist's shop sells toothpaste, bandages and medicines.

shoulder

Your shoulder is the place where your arm joins your body.

shout

You shout when you speak as loudly as you can.

show

If you show something, you let other people see it.

shower

A shower is a short burst of rain. You can also have a shower instead of a bath.

shut

When you shut your eyes, you lower your eyelids until you can't see anything.

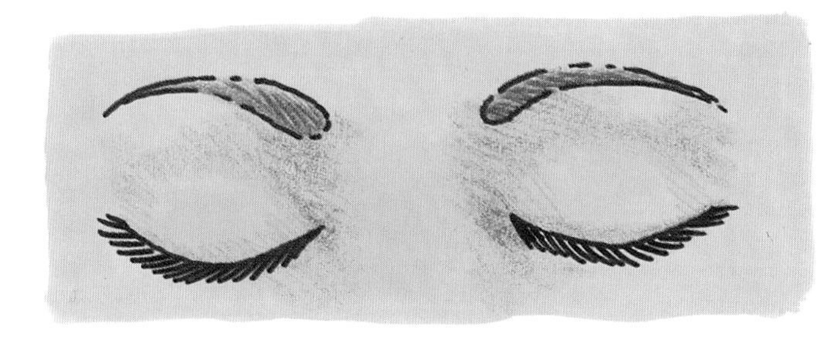

sick

When you are sick you feel ill. Have you been eating too many cakes?

sing

When you sing you make a tune with your voice.

sit

When you put your bottom on a seat or chair, you sit on it.

skirt

Girls often wear a skirt over their legs instead of trousers.

sky

Go outside and look straight upwards. You're looking at the sky.

sleep

When you sleep your body rests but your brain still works and you can dream.

slide

This park has a smooth metal slide for children to play on.

slip

If you run too fast on the snow, you could slip and fall.

slow

Something that takes a long time is slow.

small

Small means not very big. Those shoes are too small for your feet.

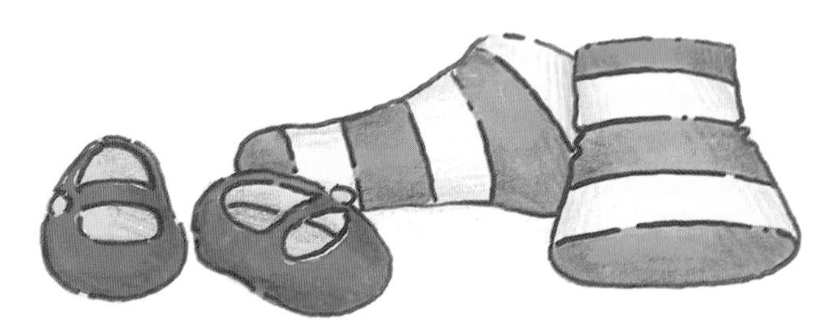

smell

We sniff with our noses to tell how things smell.

smile

When you are pleased, the corners of your mouth turn upwards in a smile.

snow
Snow is frozen rain that falls in winter. You can press it together to make a snowball or a snowman.

soap
You wash with soap and water. Soap picks up the dirt and water washes it away.

sock
You wear socks to keep your feet warm.

soft
You can easily bend or shape something that is soft. A soft chair feels very comfortable.

sore
If a part of your body is sore it hurts a lot.

soup
Soup is a liquid food that is often made from vegetables.

spell
When you know the order of the letters in a word, you can spell it.

spider
A spider is a little animal with eight legs. It eats flies and spins webs.

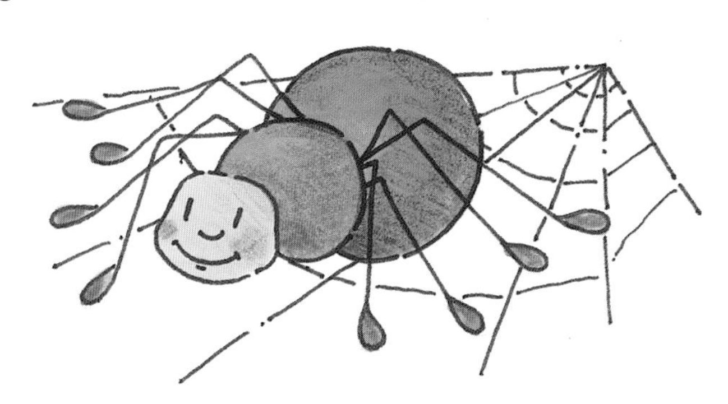

spoon

We can hold or stir food with a spoon.

stairs

Many houses have a set of steps called stairs that lead up to the bedrooms.

stamp

A stamp is a little paper picture that you stick on an envelope.

stand

Some people have to stand when there are no seats left on the bus.

star

A star is a shiny point that you can see in the sky at night.

start

This is the start of the race. You begin here.

stop

Cars must stop when the traffic lights are on red.

story

A story tells you about something that happened. It can be real or made up.

street

The road between two rows of houses is sometimes called a street.

strong
If you can lift things that are very heavy, you must be strong.

sugar
We put sugar into food or drinks to make them sweet.

summer
Summer is the warmest part of the year, when many people take their holidays.

sun
We can see the sun in the sky in the daytime. It gives us heat and light.

supermarket
A supermarket is a very big shop that sells all kinds of things.

surprise
A surprise is something you didn't expect.

sweet
Sweets have a lot of sugar in them. They are bad for your teeth.

swim
We swim by using our arms and legs to move us through the water.

swing
A swing is a seat on ropes or chains. It swings backwards and forwards.

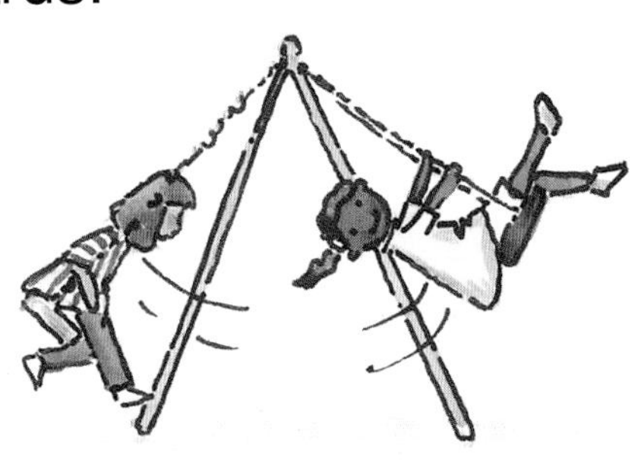

Tt

table

A table is a flat surface on legs where you can eat or work.

tall

A tall building is higher than most other buildings.

taste

The taste of something is what it feels like in your mouth.

tea

Tea is a drink that is made from boiling the dried leaves of a tea plant in water.

teacher

A teacher shows you how to do things properly. Teachers work in schools.

television

You can watch films, the news, cartoons or other programmes on a television.

tell

You can tell someone a story by reading it out of a book or by making it up.

throw

By swinging your arm through the air and letting go of the ball, you can throw it.

tie

We tie a shoelace by folding the ends together in a special way.

toe
Each of the five separate parts on the end of your foot is called a toe.

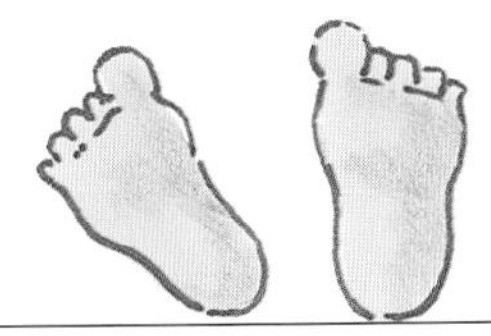

tomato
A tomato is a round red fruit with lots of yellow seeds inside. It can be eaten raw or cooked.

tongue
Your tongue is the long soft part inside your mouth that you use for tasting food.

tooth
Each of the white bony pieces inside your mouth is called a tooth. Brush your teeth!

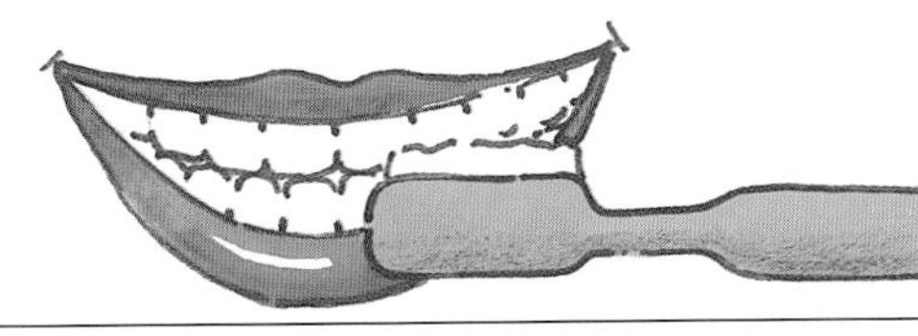

touch
If you want to know what something feels like, touch it with your fingers.

towel
A towel is a thick piece of cloth you use to dry yourself with.

toy
A toy is something that children play with, like a doll or a train set.

train
A train is a railway engine and the carriages that it pulls.

trousers
A pair of trousers covers you all the way from your waist down to your feet.

Uu

umbrella
An umbrella is made from cloth and metal. It keeps us dry when it is raining.

uniform
The special clothes that some people wear at work are their uniform. Some children wear a uniform to school.

up
When you go from the bottom of the stairs to the top, you are going up.

upside-down
Upside-down means with the top at the bottom and the bottom at the top!

Vv

van
A van is used to carry things by road. It is smaller than a lorry.

vase
A vase is a special jar that we can use for putting flowers in.

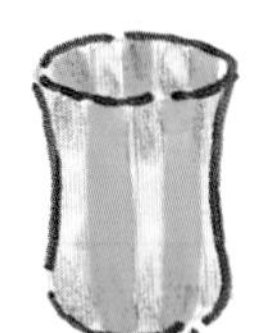

vegetable
A vegetable is a plant that we grow for food. Potatoes, carrots and onions are all vegetables.

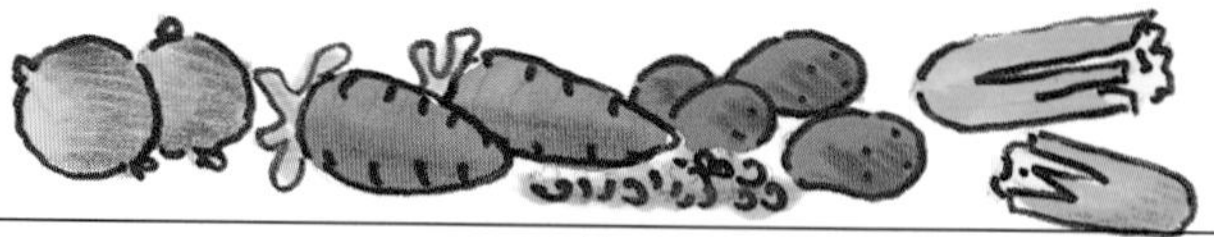

video
A video is a machine for playing tapes on television. The tapes are called videos too.

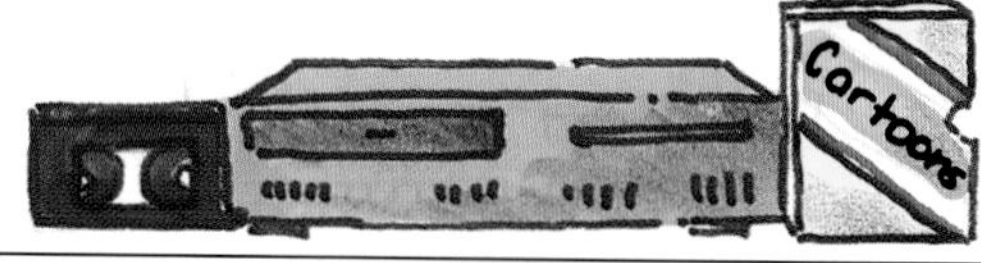

visit
When you visit someone, you go to see them at their house, or when they are in hospital.

Ww

wait
We usually have to wait at the bus stop for a while until the bus comes.

walk
When you walk, you keep putting one foot in front of the other. Walking is slower than running.

wall
A wall divides one room or house from another. It can be made from bricks, or other things.

want
When you want something, you would like to have it.

warm
When you're not too hot and not too cold, you are just warm enough.

wash
We wash our bodies and our clothes to keep them clean.

wasp
A wasp is an insect that can sting.

watch
A watch is like a small clock that you can wear on your wrist.

water
Water is a liquid. It falls from the sky as rain. It also comes out of a tap.

wave

You wave hello or goodbye to someone by shaking your hand in the air.

wear

We wear clothes when we put them on and walk around in them.

week

A week is a length of time. There are seven days in a week.

Monday	Tuesday	Wednesday	Thursday	Friday	Saturday	Sunday
	Went to school			Jo's Party		Went Fishing

weigh

When you weigh something you find out how heavy it is.

wet

Water is wet. I got wet in the rain.

wheel

A wheel is a round shape that travels along on its edge. Cars, lorries and bicycles have wheels.

whisper

When you whisper, you say something very, very quietly.

win

If you want to win a prize, you have to do better than anyone else.

wind

Wind is air that blows about outside.

window

A window is a piece of glass put in a wall so that light can come in.

wing

Birds have two wings which they flap up and down to fly.

winter

Winter is the coldest time of year, when we have snow and ice.

wish

A wish is something that you hope will happen.

woman

A woman is a girl who has grown up and is at least 18 years old.

word

A word is a small part of a sentence. It is made up of groups of letters.

work

People go to work to earn money to buy food and clothes.

write

You can use a pen or pencil to write words on a piece of paper.

wrong

"Do 1 + 1 make 3?" "No, that's wrong. The right answer is 2."

Xx

x-ray
An x-ray is a special kind of photograph that shows the inside of your body.

Yy

year
A year is a length of time. There are twelve months in a year.

yes
Yes is a word we say to agree with people.

yoghurt
Yoghurt is a kind of food that is made from milk.

young
A person or animal that is young was born not long ago.

yo-yo
A yo-yo is a wooden or plastic toy that winds itself up and down on a piece of string.

Zz

zebra
A zebra looks like a horse with black and white stripes all over. It lives in Africa.

zip
A zip is often used on trousers or jackets to fasten them up.

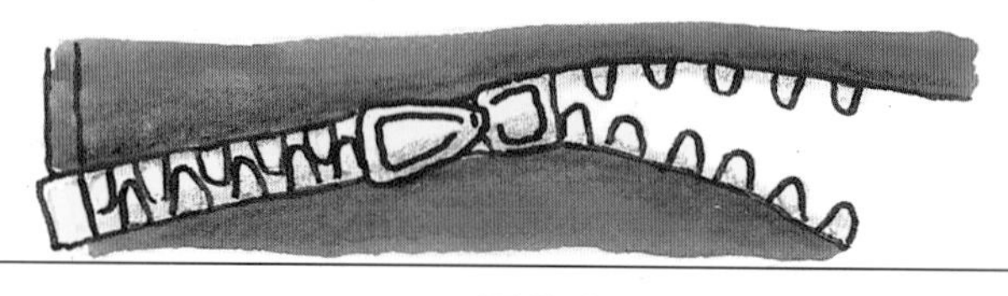

zoo
A zoo is a special park where you can see animals from all over the world.